iEdutainments Limited
The Old Post House
Radford Road
Flyford Flavell
Worcestershire
WR7 4DL
England

Company Number: 7441490
First Edition: iEdutainments Ltd 2014
Copyright © Rory Ryder 2014
Copyright © Illustrations Rory Ryder 2014
Copyright © Coloured verb tables Rory Ryder 2014

The Author asserts the moral right to be identified as the author of this work under the copyright designs and patents Act 1988.

English Version

Illustrated by Andy Garnica

All rights reserved. No part of this publication may be reproduced, stored in a retrieval system, or transmitted, in any form or by any means, electronic, mechanical, photocopying, recording or otherwise, without the prior permission of the publishers.

LEARNBOTS®
LEARN 101 CHINESE VERBS
IN 1 DAY
with the LearnBots

by Rory Ryder

Illustrations Andy Garnica

Published by:

iEdutainments Ltd.

Introduction

Memory

When learning a language, we often have problems remembering the (key) verbs; it does not mean we have totally forgotten them. It just means that we can't recall them at that particular moment. So this book has been carefully designed to help you recall the (key) verbs and their conjugations instantly.

The Research

Research has shown that one of the most effective ways to remember something is by association. Therefore we have hidden the verb (keyword) into each illustration to act as a retrieval cue that will then stimulate your long-term memory. This method has proved 7 times more effective than just passively reading and responding to a list of verbs.

Beautiful Illustrations

The LearnBot illustrations have their own mini story, an approach beyond conventional verb books. To make the most of this book, spend time with each picture and become familiar with everything that is happening. The Pictures involve the characters, Verbito, Verbita, Cyberdog and the BeeBots, with hidden clues that give more meaning to each picture. Some pictures are more challenging than others, adding to the fun but, more importantly, aiding the memory process.

Keywords

We have called the infinitive the (keyword) to refer to its central importance in remembering the 36 ways it can be used. Once you have located the appropriate keyword and made the connection with the illustration, you can then start to learn each colour-tense.

Colour-Coded Verb Tables

The verb tables are designed to save you further valuable time by focusing all your attention on one color tense allowing you to make immediate connections between the subject and verb. Making this association clear and simple from the beginning will give you more confidence to start speaking the language.

LearnBots Animations

Each picture in this book can also be viewed as an animation for FREE. Simply visit our animations link on www.LearnBots.com

Master the Verbs

Once your confident with each colour-tense, congratulate yourself because you will have learnt over 3600 verb forms, an achievement that takes some people years to master!

So is it really possible to "Learn 101 Verbs in 1 Day"?

Well, the answer to this is yes! If you carfully look at each picture and make the connection and see the (keyword) you should be able to remember the 101 verb infinitives in just one day. Of course remembering all the conjugations is going to take you longer but by at least knowing the most important verbs you can then start to learn each tense in your own time.

Reviews

Testimonials from Heads of M.F.L. & Teachers using the books with their classes around the U.K.

"This stimulating verb book, hitherto a contradiction in terms, goes a long way to dispelling the fear of putting essential grammar at the heart of language learning at the early and intermediate stages.

Particularly at the higher level of GCSE speaking and writing, where many students find themselves at a loss for a sufficient range of verbs to express what they were/ have been/ are and will be doing, these books enhances their conviction to express themselves richly, with subtlety and accuracy.

More exciting still is the rapid progress with which new (Year 8) learners both assimilate the core vocabulary and seek to speak and write about someone other than 'I'.

The website is outstanding in its accessibility and simplicity for students to listen to the recurrent patterns of all 101 verbs from someone else's voice other than mine is a significant advantage. I anticipate a more confident, productive and ambitious generation of linguists will benefit from your highly effective product."

Yours sincerely

Andy Smith, Head of Spanish, Salesian College

After a number of years in which educational trends favoured oral fluency over grammatical accuracy, it is encouraging to see a book which goes back to the basics and makes learning verbs less daunting and even easy. At the end of the day, verb patterns are fundamental in order to gain linguistic precision and sophistication, and thus should not be regarded as a chore but as necessary elements to achieve competence in any given language.

The colour coding in this book makes for quick identification of tenses, and the running stories provided by the pictures are an ideal mnemonic device in that they help students visualize each word. I would heartily recommend this fun verb book for use with pupils in the early stages of language learning and for revision later on in their school careers.

It can be used for teaching but also, perhaps more importantly, as a tool for independent study. The website stresses this fact as students can comfortably check the pronunciation guide from their own homes. This is a praiseworthy attempt to make Spanish verbs more easily accessible to every schoolboy and girl in the country.

Dr Josep-Lluís González Medina Head of Spanish
Eton College

We received the book in January with a request to review it - well, a free book is always worth it. We had our apprehensions as to how glitzy can a grammar book be? I mean don't they all promise to improve pupils' results and engage their interest?

So, imagine my shock when after three lessons with a mixed ability year 10 group, the majority of pupils could write the verb 'tener' in three tenses- past, present and future. It is the way this book colour codes each tense which makes it easy for the pupils to learn. With this success, I transferred the information onto PowerPoint and presented it at the start of each class as the register was taken, after which pupils were asked for the English of each verb. This again showed the majority of pupils had taken in the information.

I sent a letter home to parents explaining what the book entailed and prepared a one-off sample lesson for parents to attend. I had a turnout of 20 parents who were amazed at how easy the book was to use. In March, the book was put to the test of the dreaded OFSTED inspector. Unexpectedly, she came into my year 10 class as they were studying the pictures during the roll call - she looked quite stunned as to how many of the verbs the pupils were able to remember. I proceeded with my lesson and during the feedback session she praised this method and thought it was the way forward in MFL teaching.

Initially we agreed to keep the book for year 10's but year 11 was introduced to the book at Easter as a revision tool. They were tested at the start of each lesson on a particular tense and if unsure were given 20 seconds to concentrate on the coloured verb table and then reciting it. There was a remarkable improvement in each pupils progress.- I only wish we had have had access to the book before Christmas in order to aid them with their coursework- But with this said the school achieved great results. In reviewing the book I would say "No more boring grammar lessons!!! This book is a great tool to learning verbs through excellent illustrations. A must-have for all language learners."

Footnote:

We have now received the new format French and the students are finding it even easier to learn the verbs and we now have more free time.

Lynda McTier, Head of Spanish Lipson Community College

to arrest 1 抓

www.learnbots.com

抓

Pinyin / pronunciation: **zhuā**

Number of strokes: **7**

Meaning: (v.) **to grab / to catch / to arrest / to snatch**

to arrive 到

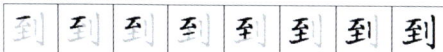

到

Pinyin / pronunciation: dào

Number of strokes: 8

Meaning: (v.) **to arrive**

to ask (for)   要

www.learnbots.com

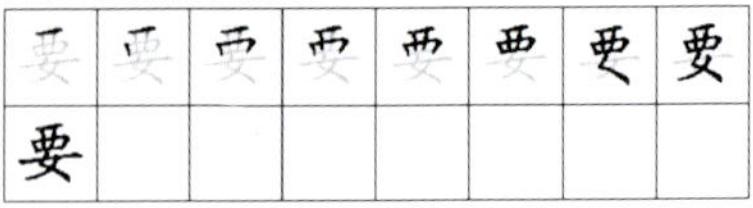

要

Pinyin / pronunciation: yāo

Number of strokes: 9

Meaning: (v.) to demand / to ask for / to request

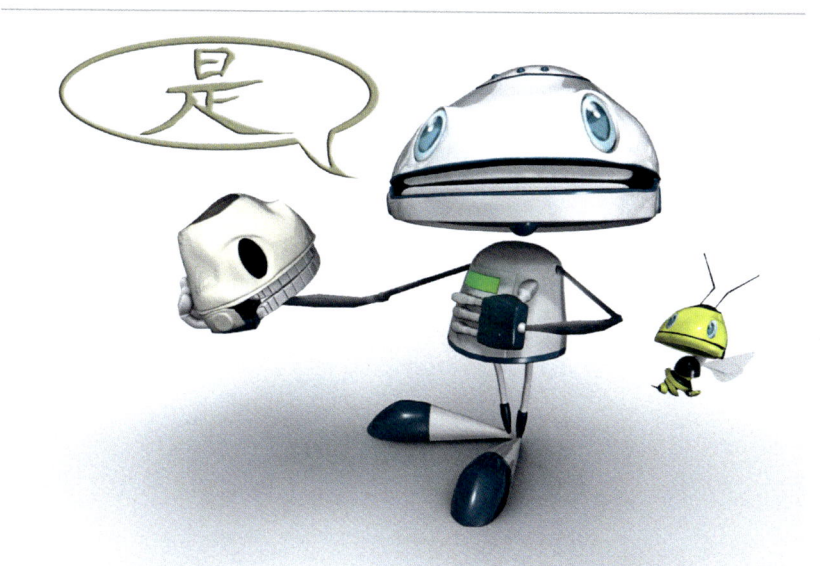

to be 是

www.learnbots.com

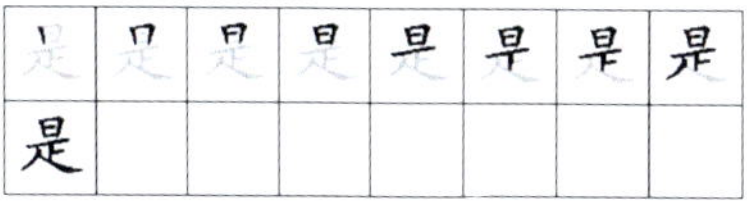

Pinyin / pronunciation: shi

Number of strokes: 9

Meaning: (v.) to be

to be   5   在

www.learnbots.com

在

Pinyin / pronunciation: **zài**

Number of strokes: **9**

Meaning: (v.) **to be**

to be able 能

www.learnbots.com

Pinyin / pronunciation: néng

Number of strokes: 10

Meaning: (v.) to be able to

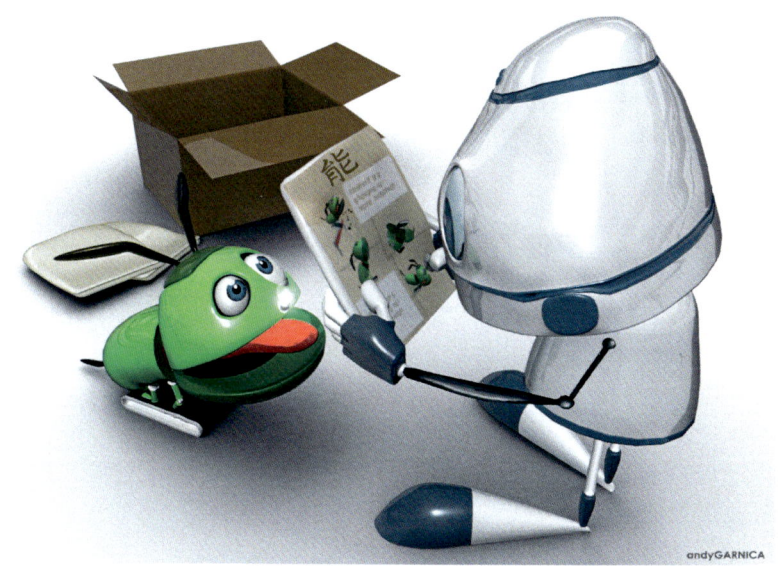

to be quiet   7   静

静

Pinyin / pronunciation: **jíng**

Number of strokes: **14**

Meaning: (v.) **to be calm / to be quiet**

to bring 带

www.learnbots.com

Pinyin / pronunciation: **dái**

Number of strokes: **9**

Meaning: (v.) **to carry / to bring**

to build 造

www.learnbots.com

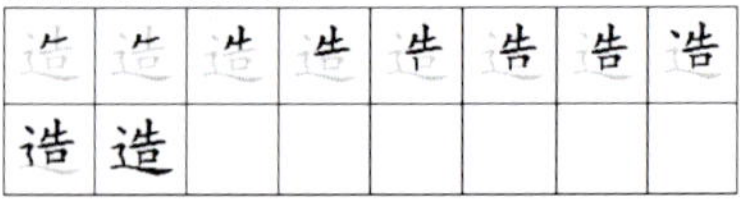

Pinyin / pronunciation: **zào**

Number of strokes: **10**

Meaning: (v.) **to establish / to build / to construct**

to buy 买

一 二 三 买 买 买

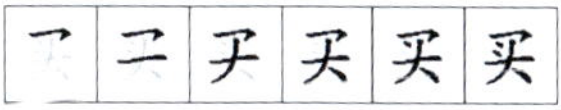

买

Pinyin / pronunciation: mǎi

Number of strokes: 6

Meaning: (v.) **to buy**

to call 11 叫

www.learnbots.com

叫

Pinyin / pronunciation: **jiào**

Number of strokes: **5**

Meaning: (v.) **to call**

to carry 拿

www.learnbots.com

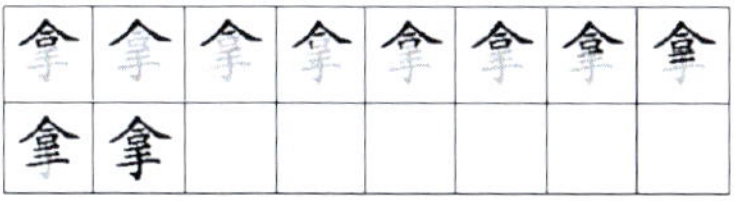

Pinyin / pronunciation: ná

Number of strokes: 10

Meaning: (v.) **to carry / to hold / to seize / to catch / to take**

to change 换

www.learnbots.com

换

Pinyin / pronunciation: huàn

Number of strokes: 10

Meaning: (v.) to change / to exchange

to clean 打扫

打扫

Pinyin / pronunciation: **dǎo sǎo**

Number of strokes: **5 + 6**

Meaning: (v.) **to clean / to sweep**

to close 15 关

www.learnbots.com

关

Pinyin / pronunciation: **guān**

Number of strokes: **6**

Meaning: (v.) **to close**

to comb 16 梳

Pinyin / pronunciation: **shū**

Number of strokes: **11**

Meaning: (v.) **to comb**

to come 17 来

来

Pinyin / pronunciation: **lái**

Number of strokes: **7**

Meaning: (v.) **to come**

to cook 煮

煮

Pinyin / pronunciation: **zhǔ**

Number of strokes: **12**

Meaning: (v.) **to cook / to boil**

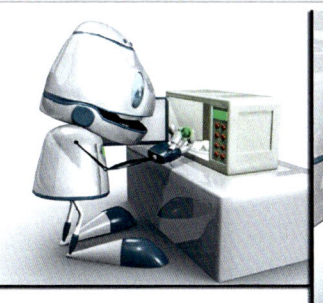

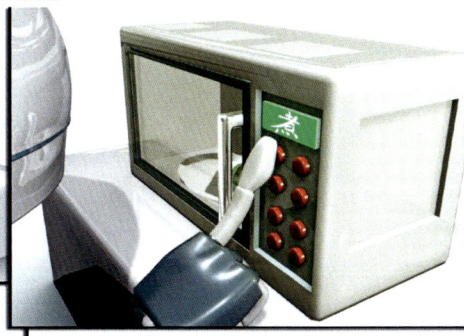

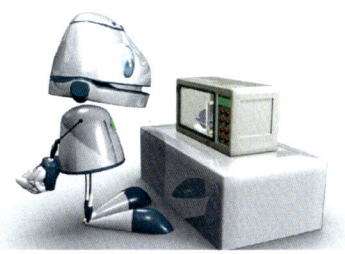

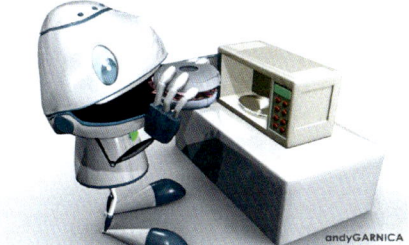

to count 数

数

Pinyin / pronunciation: shǔ

Number of strokes: 13

Meaning: (v.) to count

to crash

坠

www.learnbots.com

坠

Pinyin / pronunciation: zhuì

Number of strokes: 7

Meaning: (v.) **to crash**

to create 创

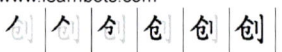

创

Pinyin / pronunciation: chuàng

Number of strokes: 6

Meaning: (v.) to begin / to initiate / to inaugurate / to start / to create

to cut — 剪

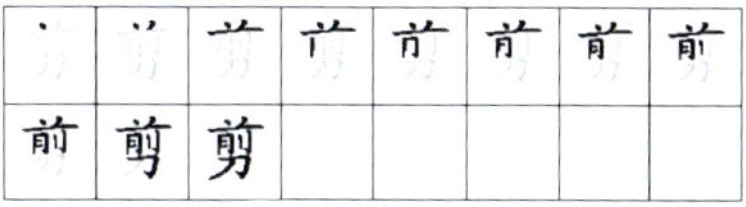

剪

Pinyin / pronunciation: **jiǎn**

Number of strokes: **11**

Meaning: (v.) **to cut**

to dance

舞

www.learnbots.com

舞

Pinyin / pronunciation: wǔ

Number of strokes:

Meaning: (v.) to dance / to wield

to decide 决定

www.learnbots.com

决定

Pinyin / pronunciation: **jué dìng**

Number of strokes: **6+8**

Meaning: (v.) **to decide (to do something)** / to determine / to resolve

to direct

导

www.learnbots.com

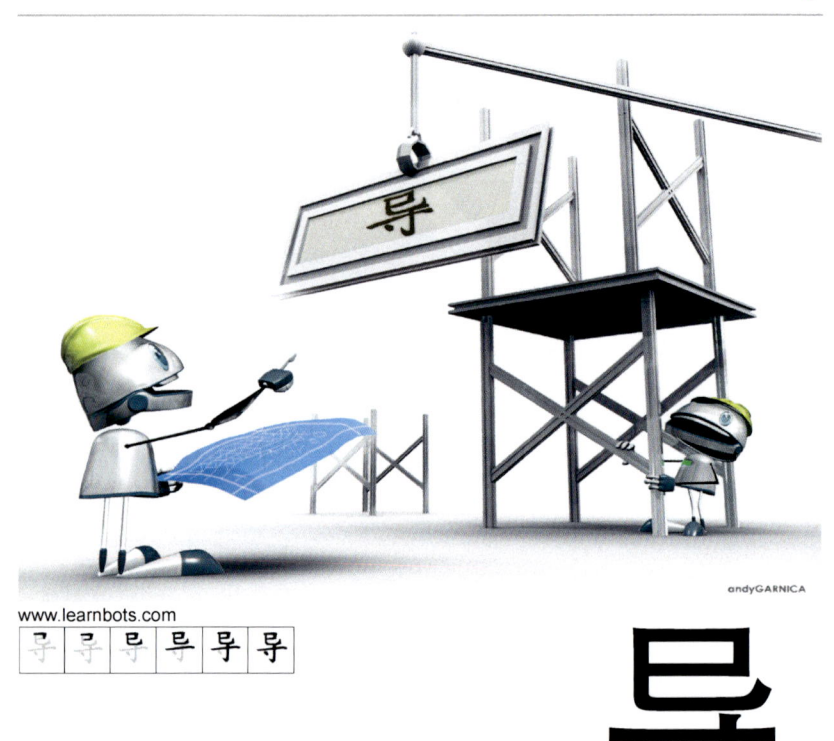

Pinyin / pronunciation: **dǎo**

Number of strokes: **6**

Meaning: (v.) **to transmit / to lead / to guide / to conduct / to direct**

to dream   梦

www.learnbots.com

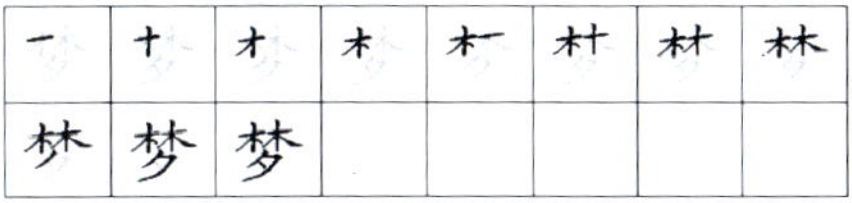

Pinyin / pronunciation: mèng

Number of strokes: 11

Meaning: (v.) to dream

to drink 喝

www.learnbots.com

喝

Pinyin / pronunciation: hē

Number of strokes: 12

Meaning: (v.) to drink

to drive 驾

28

www.learnbots.com

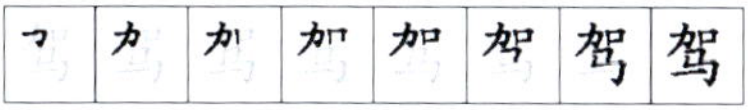

| フ | カ | カ⁀ | カ⼍ | 加 | architecture | 驾 | 驾 |

驾

Pinyin / pronunciation: jià

Number of strokes: 8

Meaning: (v.) to drive / to draw / to harness / to mount

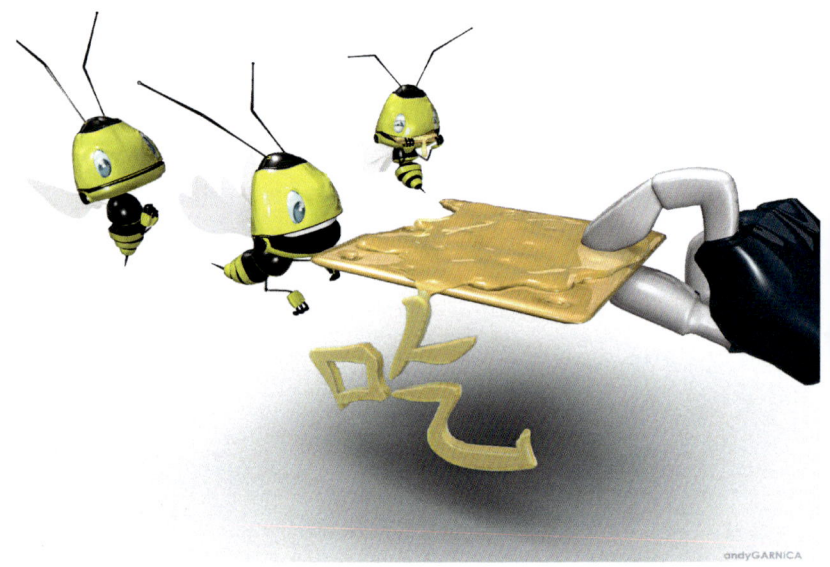

to eat   29   吃

www.learnbots.com

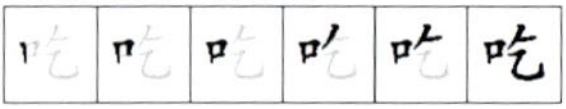

吃

Pinyin / pronunciation: **chī**

Number of strokes: **6**

Meaning: (v.) **to eat**

to enter 進

www.learnbots.com

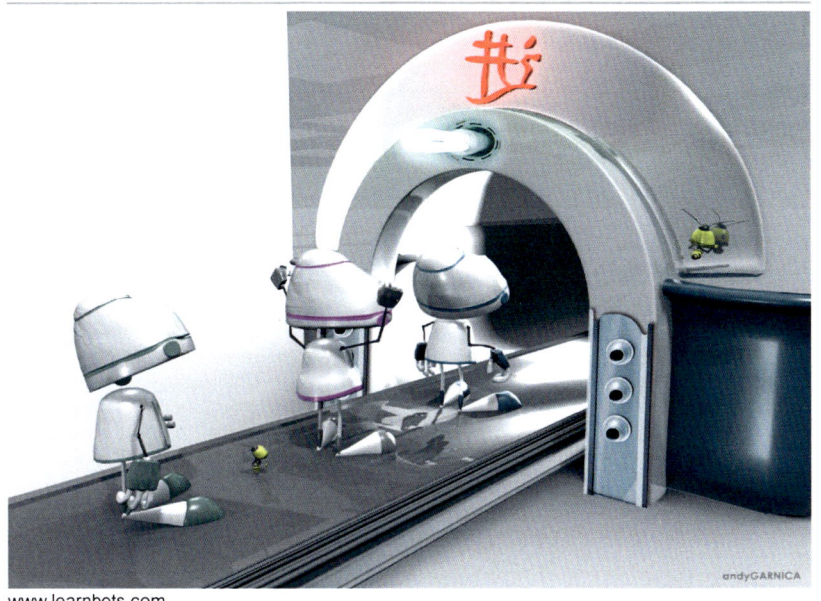

進

Pinyin / pronunciation: **jìn**

Number of strokes: **7**

Meaning: (v.) **to advance / to enter / to come in**

to fall 掉

www.learnbots.com

掉

Pinyin / pronunciation: **diào**

Number of strokes: **11**

Meaning: (v.) **to drop / to fall**

to fight — 打

打

www.learnbots.com

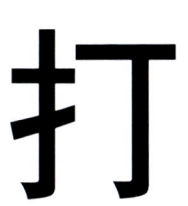

Pinyin / pronunciation: **dǎ**

Number of strokes: **5**

Meaning: (v.) **to beat / to strike / to break / to fight**

to find 找到

找到

Pinyin / pronunciation: **zhǎo dào**

Number of strokes: **7 + 8**

Meaning: (v.) **to find (what one was searching for)**

to finish 结束

Pinyin / pronunciation: **jié shù**

Number of strokes: 9 + 7

Meaning: (v.) **to finish** / to end / to conclude / to close

to follow 35 跟

www.learnbots.com

andyGARNICA

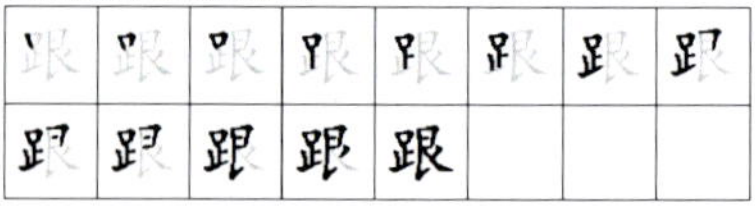

跟

Pinyin / pronunciation: **gēn**

Number of strokes: **13**

Meaning: (v.) **to follow**

to forbid 禁

Pinyin / pronunciation: jìn

Number of strokes: 13

Meaning: (v.) **to prohibit / to forbit / to ban**

to forget 37 忘

忘

Pinyin / pronunciation: **wàng**

Number of strokes: **7**

Meaning: (v.) **to forget / to overlook / to neglect**

to get dressed 穿

www.learnbots.com

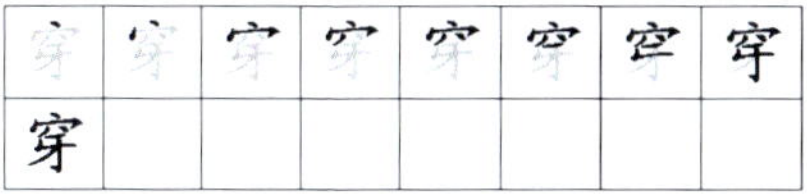

穿

Pinyin / pronunciation: **chuān**

Number of strokes: **9**

Meaning: (v.) **to dress**

to get married 结婚

结婚

Pinyin / pronunciation: jié hūn

Number of strokes: 11

Meaning: (v.) **to marry / to get married**

to give 给

www.learnbots.com

ノ	ㄥ	纟	纠	纠	纟	纟	给
给							

给

Pinyin / pronunciation: **gěi**

Number of strokes: **9**

Meaning: (v.) **to give**

to go — 41 — 去

www.learnbots.com

去

Pinyin / pronunciation: **qù**

Number of strokes: **5**

Meaning: (v.) **to go / to leave / to remove**

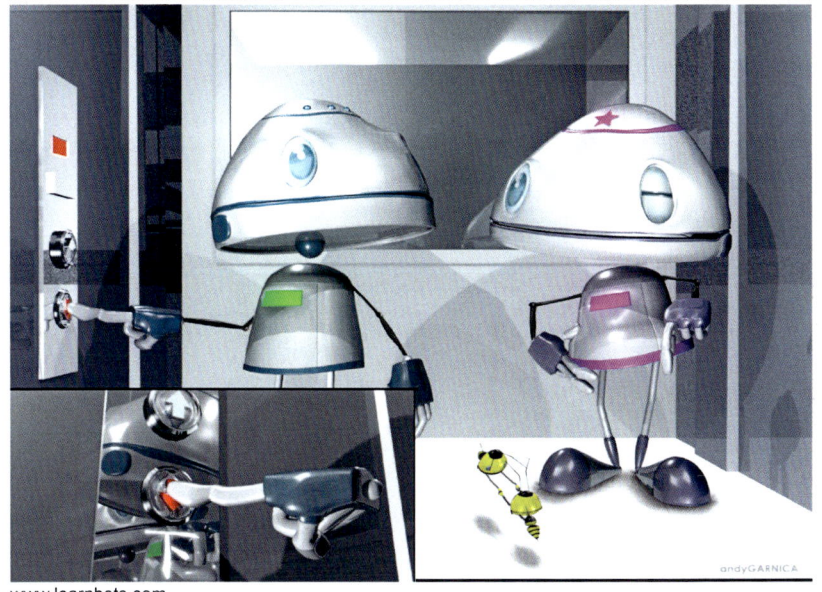

to go down 42 下

下

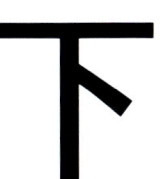

Pinyin / pronunciation: **xià**

Number of strokes: **3**

Meaning: (v.) **to go down / to decline**

to go out 43 离

www.learnbots.com

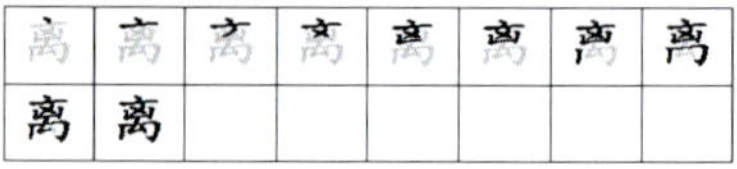

离

Pinyin / pronunciation: **lí**

Number of strokes: **10**

Meaning: (v.) **to leave / to depart / to go away**

to grow 44 长

www.learnbots.com

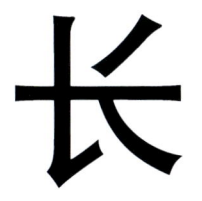

长

Pinyin / pronunciation: **zhǎng**

Number of strokes: **4**

Meaning: (v.) **to grow / to develop**

to have 有

www.learnbots.com

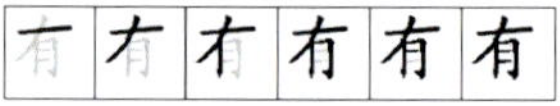

有

Pinyin / pronunciation: yǒu

Number of strokes: 6

Meaning: (v.) to have

to hear 46 听

www.learnbots.com

听

Pinyin / pronunciation: **tīng**

Number of strokes: **7**

Meaning: (v.) **to listen / to hear / to obey**

to jump 47 跳

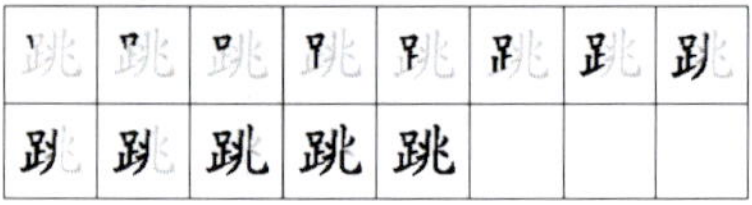

跳

Pinyin / pronunciation: **tiào**

Number of strokes: **13**

Meaning: (v.) **to jump / to hop / to skip (a grade) / to bounce / to beat**

to kick

踢

www.learnbots.com

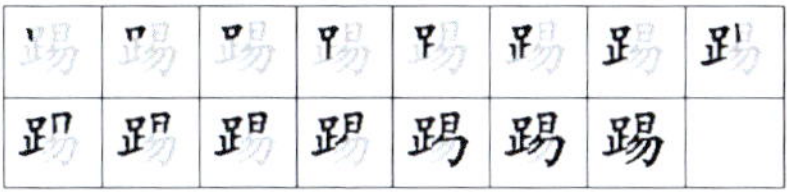

踢

Pinyin / pronunciation: **tī**

Number of strokes: **15**

Meaning: (v.) **to kick / to play (football or soccer)**

to kiss 49 吻

www.learnbots.com

吻

Pinyin / pronunciation: **wěn**

Number of strokes: **7**

Meaning: (v.) **to kiss**

to know   知

知

Pinyin / pronunciation: **zhī**

Number of strokes: **8**

Meaning: (v.) **to know / to be aware**

to learn   51   学习

www.learnbots.com

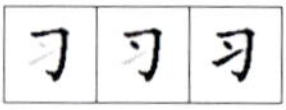

丨 刁 习

学习

Pinyin / pronunciation: **xí**

Number of strokes: **3**

Meaning: (v.) **to practice / to study**

to lie   谎报

谎报

Pinyin / pronunciation: **shuō huǎng**

Number of strokes: **9 + 11**

Meaning: (v.) **to lie**

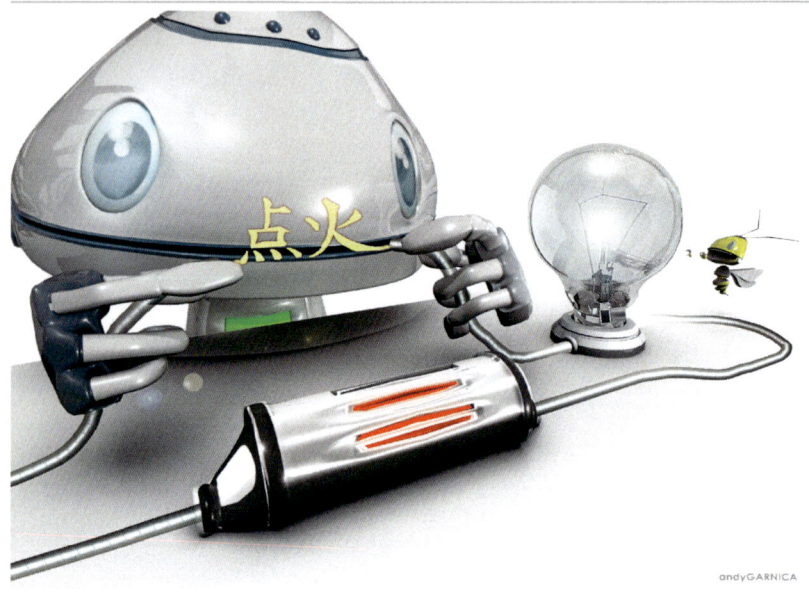

to light 火

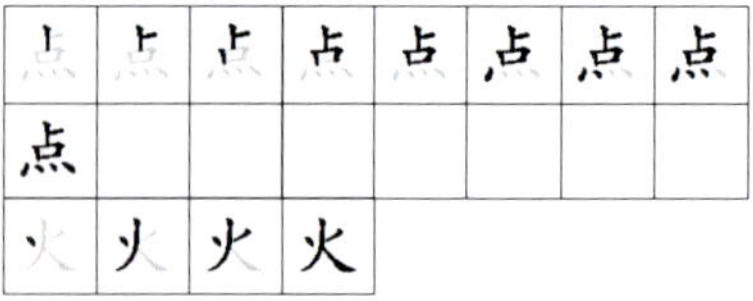

火

Pinyin / pronunciation: diǎn huǒ

Number of strokes: 9 + 4

Meaning: (v.) to make a fire / to light a fire

to like 54 喜欢

喜欢

Pinyin / pronunciation: **xǐ huǎn**

Number of strokes: **12 + 6**

Meaning: (v.) **to like / to be fond of**

to lose

输

Pinyin / pronunciation: **shū**

Number of strokes: **13**

Meaning: (v.) **to lose**

to love 爱

www.learnbots.com

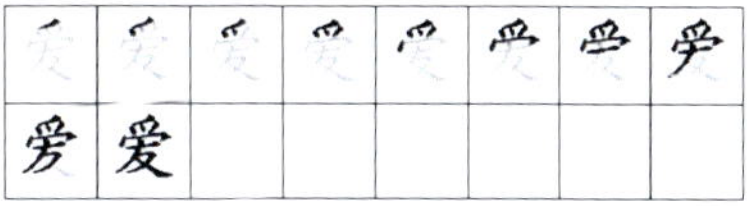

爱

Pinyin / pronunciation: ài

Number of strokes: 10

Meaning: (v.) **to love / to be fond of / to like**

to make 57 造

造

Pinyin / pronunciation: **ná**

Number of strokes: **11**

Meaning: (v.) **to do / to make / to produce**

to open 开

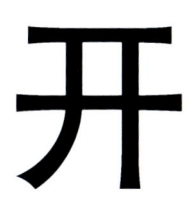

开

Pinyin / pronunciation: **kāi**

Number of strokes: **4**

Meaning: (v.) **to open**

to organise 整理

Pinyin / pronunciation: **zhěng lǐ**

Number of strokes: **16 + 11**

Meaning: (v.) **to arrange / to organise**

to paint 画

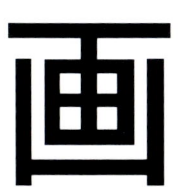

画

Pinyin / pronunciation: **huà**

Number of strokes: **8**

Meaning: (v.) **to draw / to paint**

to pay   付

付

Pinyin / pronunciation: **fù**

Number of strokes: **5**

Meaning: (v.) **to pay**

to play 玩

www.learnbots.com

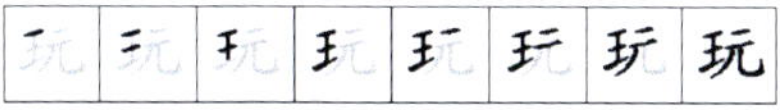

玩

Pinyin / pronunciation: **wán**

Number of strokes: **8**

Meaning: (v.) **to play / to amuse oneself**

to polish

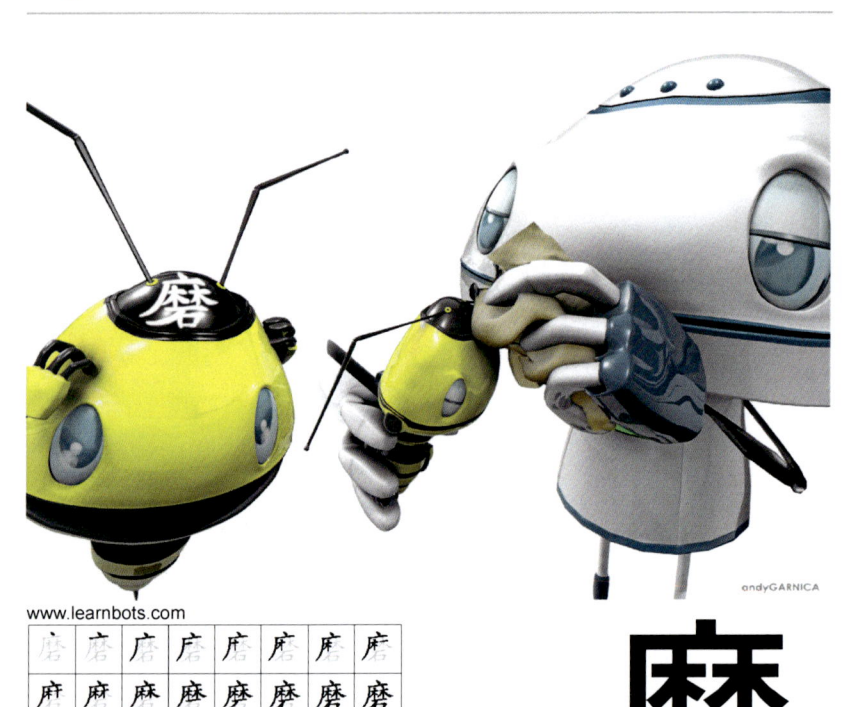

磨

Pinyin / pronunciation: **mó**

Number of strokes: **16**

Meaning: (v.) **to polish**

to put 放

www.learnbots.com

放

Pinyin / pronunciation: **fàng**

Number of strokes: **8**

Meaning: (v.) **to release / to free / to let go / to put / to place / to let out**

to quit   戒

戒

Pinyin / pronunciation: **jiè**

Number of strokes: **7**

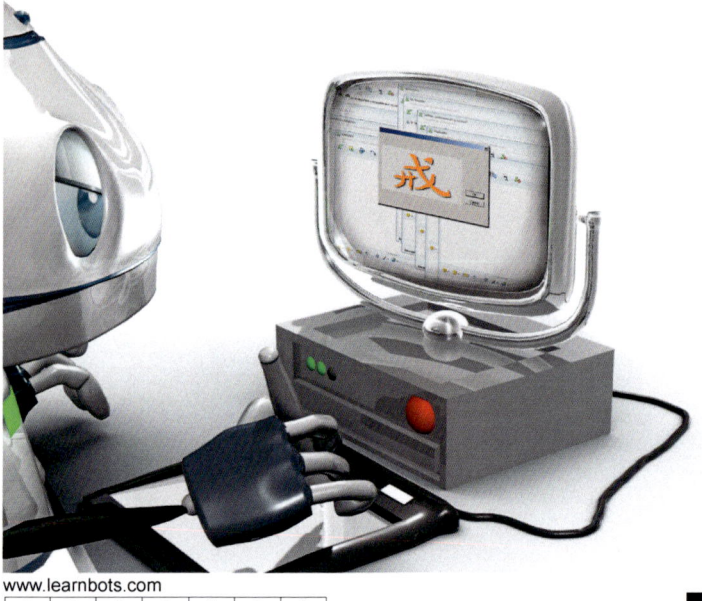

Meaning: (v.) **to swear off / to warn against / to quit**

to rain   雨

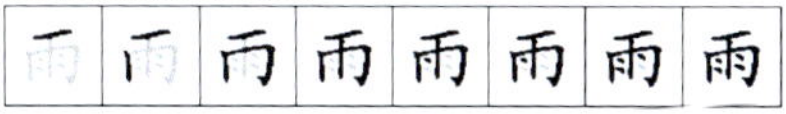

雨

Pinyin / pronunciation: **yǔ**

Number of strokes: **8**

Meaning: (v.) **to rain**

to read 读

读

Pinyin / pronunciation: dú

Number of strokes: 10

Meaning: (v.) to read / to study

to receive 68 收

www.learnbots.com

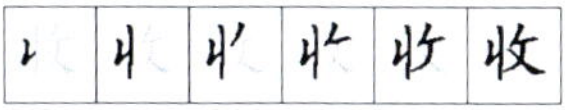

收

Pinyin / pronunciation: **shōu**

Number of strokes: **6**

Meaning: (v.) **to receive / to accept / to collect**

to record 录

录

Pinyin / pronunciation: **lù**

Number of strokes: **8**

Meaning: (v.) **to record / to copy**

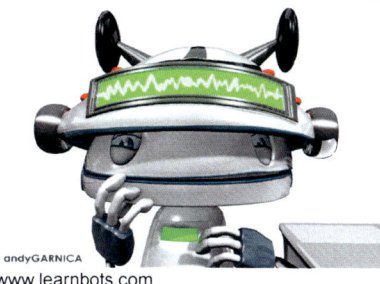

to remember 70 记

记

Pinyin / pronunciation: **jì**

Number of strokes: **5**

Meaning: (v.) **to remember / to note / to mark / to sign / to record**

to repair 修

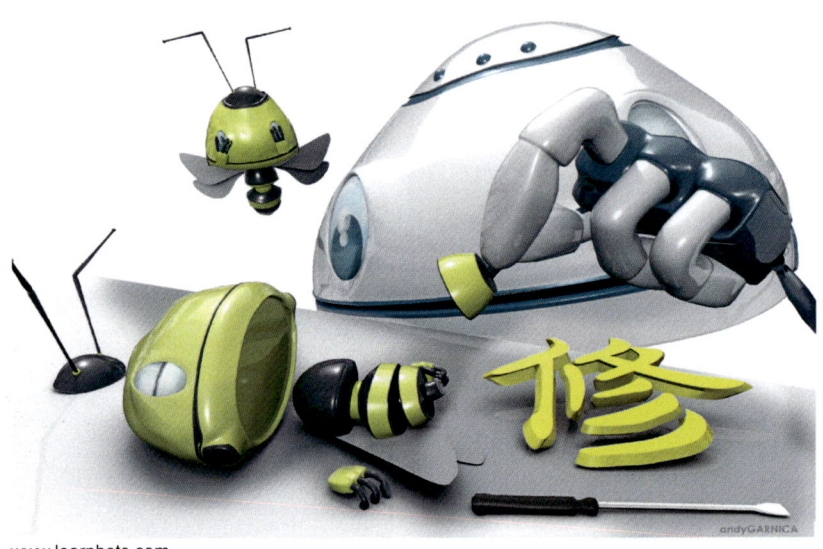

www.learnbots.com

修

Pinyin / pronunciation: xiū

Number of strokes: 9

Meaning: (v.) to repair

to return

72

回

www.learnbots.com

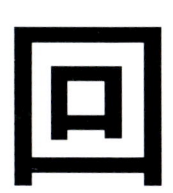

Pinyin / pronunciation: **huí**

Number of strokes: **6**

Meaning: (v.) **to return / to go back**

to run 跑

www.learnbots.com

跑

Pinyin / pronunciation: pǎo

Number of strokes: 12

Meaning: (v.) to run / to escape

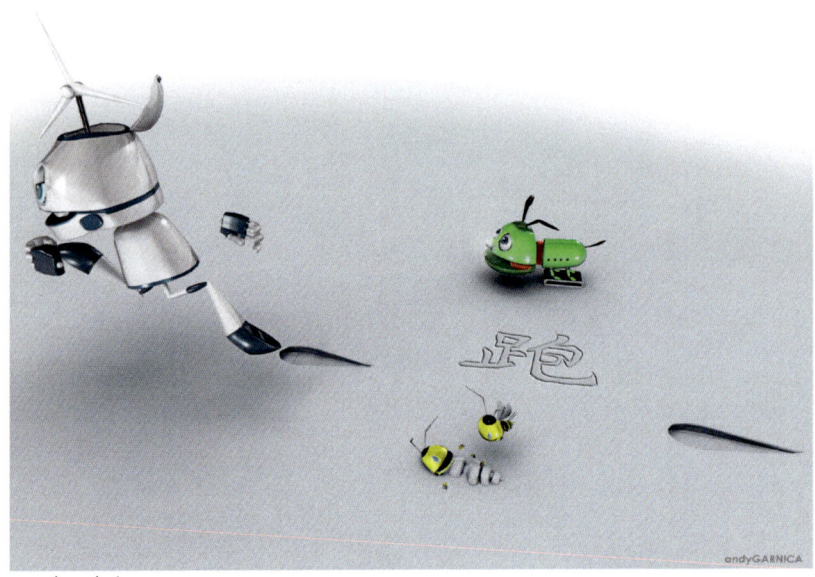

to scream 喊

www.learnbots.com

Pinyin / pronunciation: hǎn

Number of strokes: 12

Meaning: (v.) to call / to cry / to shout / to scream

to search 75 找

www.learnbots.com

找

Pinyin / pronunciation: **zhǎo**

Number of strokes: **7**

Meaning: (v.) **to try to find / to look for / to search**

to see 见

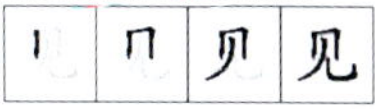

见

Pinyin / pronunciation: jiàn

Number of strokes: 4

Meaning: (v.) to see / to meet / to appear / to interview

to separate

分

www.learnbots.com

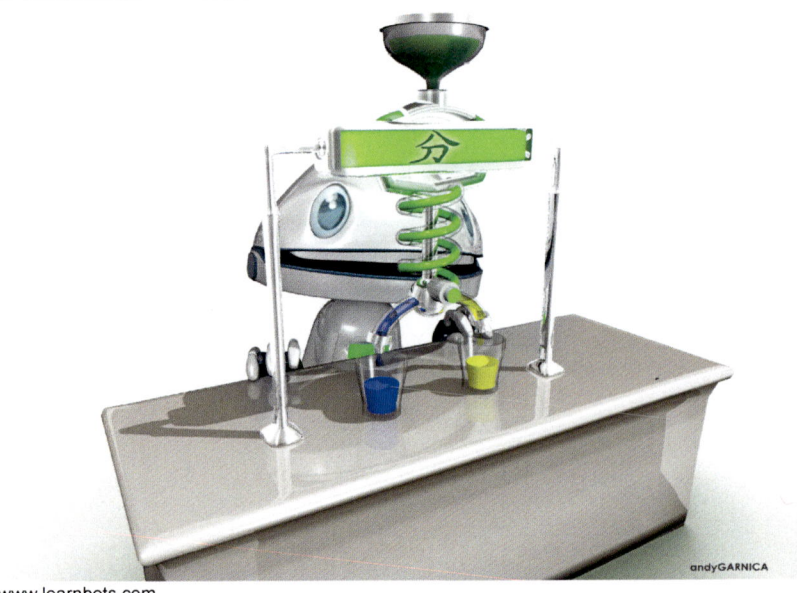

Pinyin / pronunciation: **fēn**

Number of strokes: **4**

Meaning: (v.) **to divide / to separate**

to show 示

示

Pinyin / pronunciation: **shì**

Number of strokes: **5**

Meaning: (v.) **to show** / **to reveal**

to shower 洗

洗

Pinyin / pronunciation: **xǐ**

Number of strokes: **9**

Meaning: (v.) **to wash / to bathe / to take a shower**

to sing   唱

唱

Pinyin / pronunciation: **chàng**

Number of strokes: **11**

Meaning: (v.) **to sing** / also means: **to call loudly** / **to chant**

to sit 　　　　　　　　　　　81　　　　　　　　　　　坐

www.learnbots.com

坐

Pinyin / pronunciation: **zuò**

Number of strokes: **7**

Meaning: (v.) **to sit / to take a sit / to take (a bus, airplane, etc)**

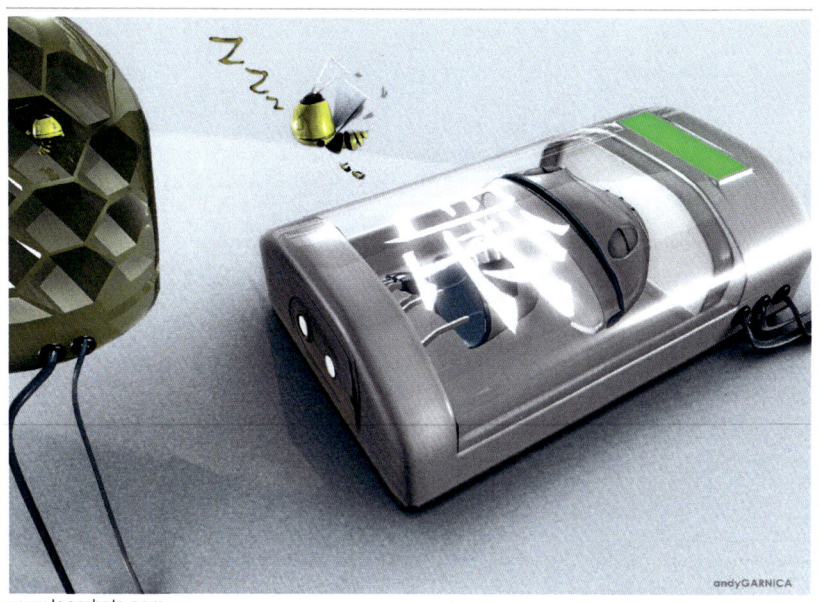

to sleep

睡

www.learnbots.com

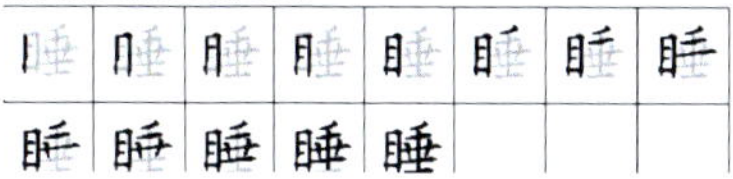

睡

Pinyin / pronunciation: shuì

Number of strokes: 13

Meaning: (v.) to sleep

to start 开始

开 始

www.learnbots.com

Pinyin / pronunciation: **kāi shǐ**

Number of strokes: **4 + 8**

Meaning: (v.) **to begin / to start**

to stop 停

www.learnbots.com

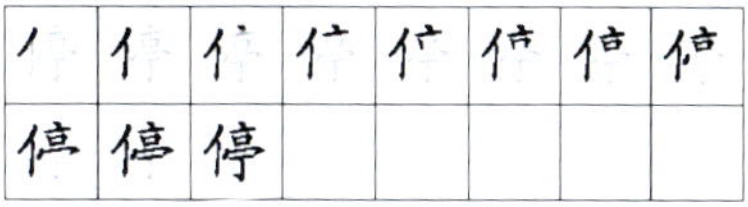

停

Pinyin / pronunciation: tíng

Number of strokes: 11

Meaning: (v.) **to stop / to halt**

to stroll 逛

逛

Pinyin / pronunciation: **guàng**

Number of strokes: **10**

Meaning: (v.) **to stroll / to walk / to visit**

to study 学

学

Pinyin / pronunciation: xué

Number of strokes: 8

Meaning: (v.) **to study**

to swim 游

游

Pinyin / pronunciation: **yóu**

Number of strokes: **12**

Meaning: (v.) **to swim / to travel**

to talk   88   说

www.learnbots.com

说

Pinyin / pronunciation: **shuō**

Number of strokes: **9**

Meaning: (v.) **to speak / to say / to talk**

to test 验

验

Pinyin / pronunciation: yàn

Number of strokes: 10

Meaning: (v.) to examine / to test / to check

to think

想

一 十 才 木 机 机 相 相 相 想 想 想 想

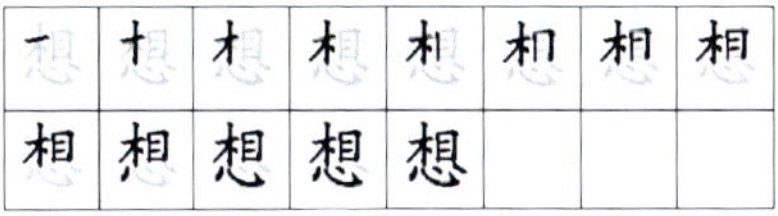

想

Pinyin / pronunciation: **xiǎng**

Number of strokes: **13**

Meaning: (v.) **to think / to believe / to suppose**

to travel 91 游

游

Pinyin / pronunciation: **lǚ yóu**

Number of strokes: **10**

Meaning: (v.) **to take a trip / to travel**

to trip — 绊

www.learnbots.com

| 乡 | 纟 | 纟 | 纟 | 纟 | 纟 | 纟 | 绊 |

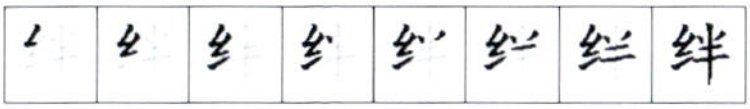

绊

Pinyin / pronunciation: **bàn**

Number of strokes: **8**

Meaning: (v.) **to trip / to stumble / to hinder**

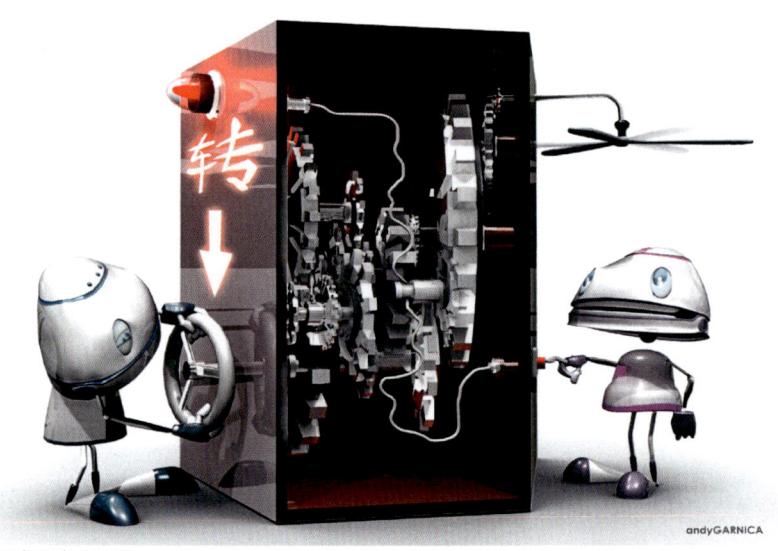

to turn 93 转

www.learnbots.com

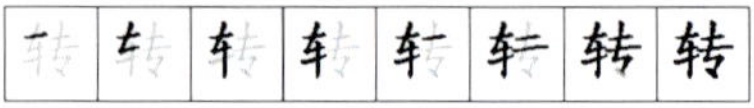

转

Pinyin / pronunciation: **zhuàn**

Number of strokes: **8**

Meaning: (v.) **to turn**

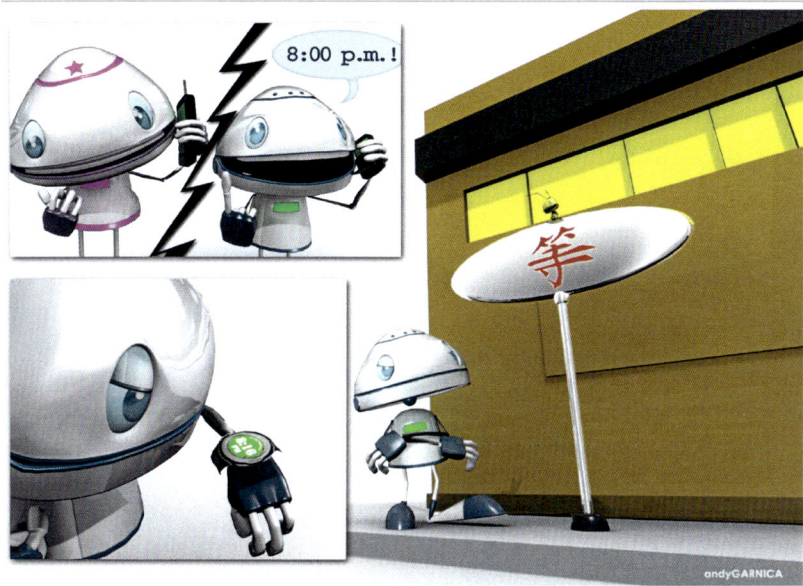

to wait 等

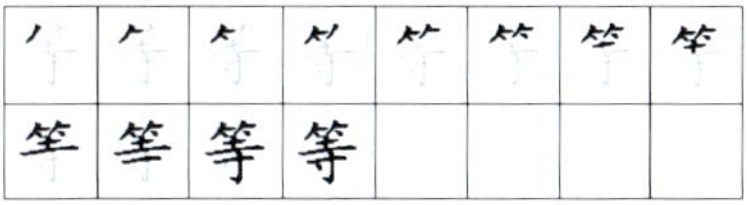

等

Pinyin / pronunciation: děng

Number of strokes: 12

Meaning: (v.) to wait

to wake up

醒

www.learnbots.com

醒

Pinyin / pronunciation: xǐng

Number of strokes: 16

Meaning: (v.) to wake up / to be awake

to walk 走

www.learnbots.com

走

Pinyin / pronunciation: **zǒu**

Number of strokes: **7**

Meaning: (v.) **to walk** / **to go** / **to move**

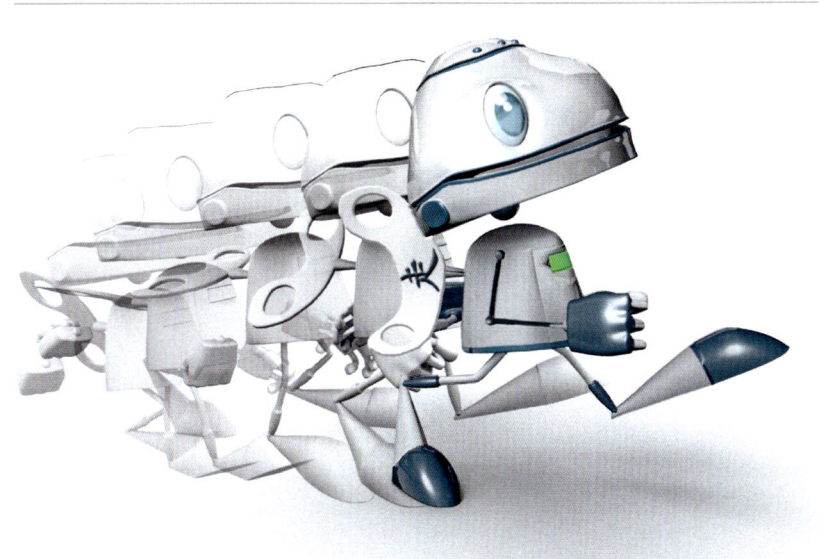

to want 想要

www.learnbots.com

想要

Pinyin / pronunciation: **xiăng yào**

Number of strokes: **13 + 9**

Meaning: (v.) **to want / to feel like**

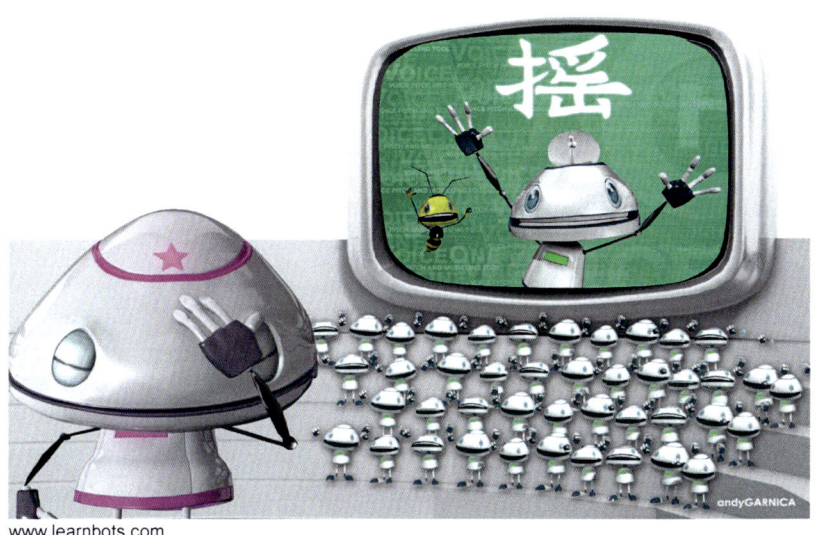

to wave / 摇

www.learnbots.com

Pinyin / pronunciation: yáo

Number of strokes: 13

Meaning: (v.) **to wave / to shake**

to watch 99 看

www.learnbots.com

看

Pinyin / pronunciation: **kān**

Number of strokes: **9**

Meaning: (v.) **to look after / to take care of / to watch / to guard**

to win 100 赢

赢

Pinyin / pronunciation: **yíng**

Number of strokes: **17**

Meaning: (v.) **to beat / to win / to profit**

to write 101 写

写

Pinyin / pronunciation: **xiě**

Number of strokes: **5**

Meaning: (v.) **to write**